for all the big ones out there
trying to build the dream life
for their little ones

ISBN 978-1-9192887-2-7

THIS BOOK BELONGS TO

LITTLE
BLOSSOM'S
BIG
MOVE

Little Blossom and Mum were in the middle of a *very* long drive.
"...something beginning with B." said Mum, tapping her fingers on the steering wheel, smiling over at Little Blossom.
"B - B - blue sky?" Little Blossom guessed hopefully, looking out of the window.
"Nope."
"Ermmm blue car?"
"Nope, I'll give you a hint, it's not blue anything."
"Oh...is it me?!" Blossom squealed, thinking she'd definitely got it this time.
"Good guess – but nope," laughed Mum, "give up yet?"

"Umm..." Blossom stammered, scanning everything she could see. There wasn't much, just the motorway with cars zooming past. There were trees and fields on the sides, haybales and sometimes sheep, but nothing starting with B! She was stumped. "Yeah, okay."

"Bumper!" smiled Mum, pleased she'd finally won one. "The B is for bumper, that great big bumper on the back of our moving van!"
"Ohh!" Blossom yawned, "good job Mum."

"Thanks sweetie," Mum chuckled, noticing Blossom yawning again. "LB sweetheart, we've still got a long way to go yet, why don't you take a little nap - you can wake up nice and fresh at our new house?"
"Hmm, yeah okay," she agreed, her eyes already closing. "I can't wait to get there!"

It was true, Blossom was very excited about moving. Her and Mum loved adventures and moving to a whole new place was their biggest one so far! But as she drifted off to sleep, she couldn't help but think about all the amazing times they had at their old home. She couldn't help but feel a little bit worried that their new house wouldn't be the same, wouldn't be as fun or feel as magical…

Like the fairy walks her and Mum often took together. Their old home was right next to a magnificent river, surrounded by wildflowers – it even had a bridge crossing.

Mum and Blossom would walk, skip and run by the river happily, collecting a few small flowers to drop over the side of the bridge.

They'd hold hands, make a wish and rush to the other side to see the flowers floating away, carrying their wishes with them.

The dragonflies (who Blossom knew were really fairies) would fly along the riverbank following them almost all the way back home.

When they got back, Blossom and Mum would head straight to the garden, lie down on the trampoline, and watch all the leaves from the trees swaying in the wind...

What if the fairies didn't live near the new house?

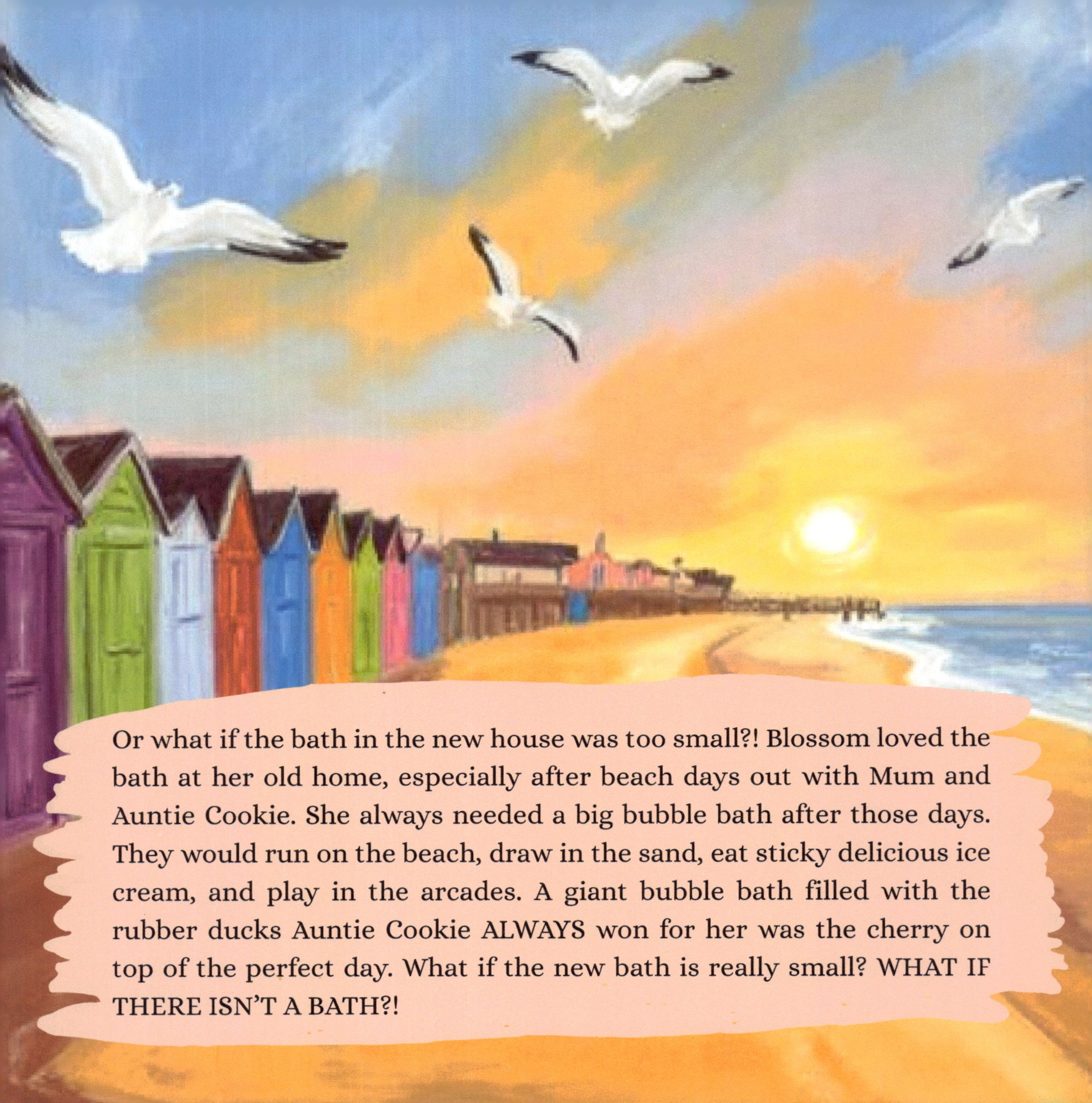
Or what if the bath in the new house was too small?! Blossom loved the bath at her old home, especially after beach days out with Mum and Auntie Cookie. She always needed a big bubble bath after those days. They would run on the beach, draw in the sand, eat sticky delicious ice cream, and play in the arcades. A giant bubble bath filled with the rubber ducks Auntie Cookie ALWAYS won for her was the cherry on top of the perfect day. What if the new bath is really small? WHAT IF THERE ISN'T A BATH?!

And the stairs?! The stairs at their old place were open from the living room, they had slats perfect for tying blankets to and a big space underneath where she and her cousins would build cosy forts.
They would spend hours playing together in the wonderful worlds they'd created.

In fact, the whole house was perfectly suited to Blossom. She loved the playdates with friends there, holiday sleepovers with Nanna and talking to her neighbours (who always loved to see her). Blossom started to grumble in her sleep, even though she *was* excited about this new adventure, she was really going to miss her old home, and everyone in it.

"LB sweetie," Mum called to her softly, "Blossom? LB?"
"Mmm."
"Open your eyes darling, you'll want to see this!"
Blossom rubbed at her eyes, the yawn that was escaping from her quickly turning into a gasp of wonder.

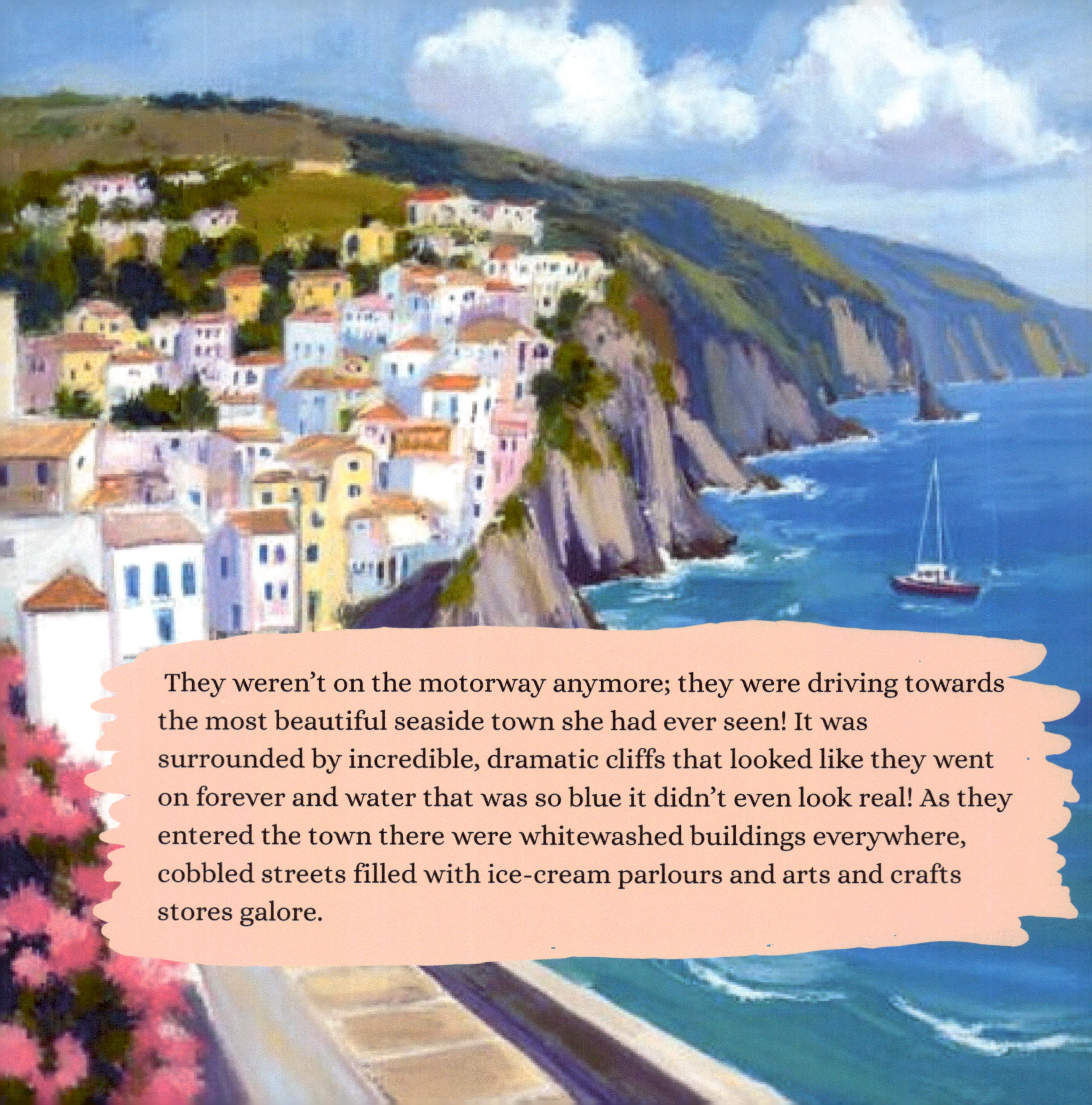

They weren't on the motorway anymore; they were driving towards the most beautiful seaside town she had ever seen! It was surrounded by incredible, dramatic cliffs that looked like they went on forever and water that was so blue it didn't even look real! As they entered the town there were whitewashed buildings everywhere, cobbled streets filled with ice-cream parlours and arts and crafts stores galore.

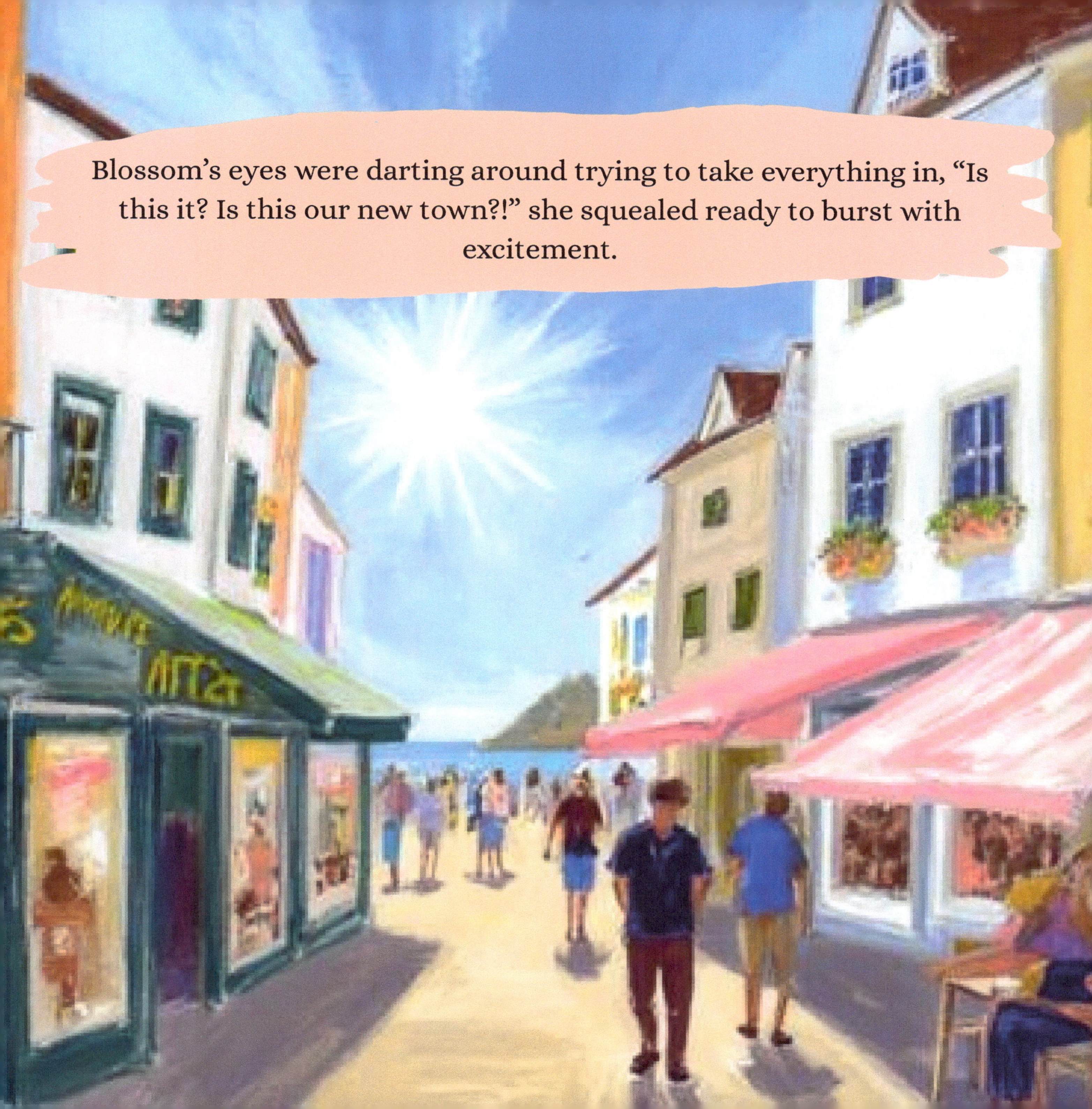

Blossom's eyes were darting around trying to take everything in, "Is this it? Is this our new town?!" she squealed ready to burst with excitement.

"It is," beamed Mum, "what do you think?"
"It's amazing!! It's so beautiful I can't believe it!"
As they kept driving, Blossom could feel all the worry that had just been sitting in her chest being replaced by happiness. She was wiggling her feet about lightning fast, itching to get to the new house and see where they would be living.

In no time they were pulling into a driveway outside of *the cutest cottage.* It was a bit smaller than their old house, but Blossom thought that how dainty and sweet it looked was just as good!

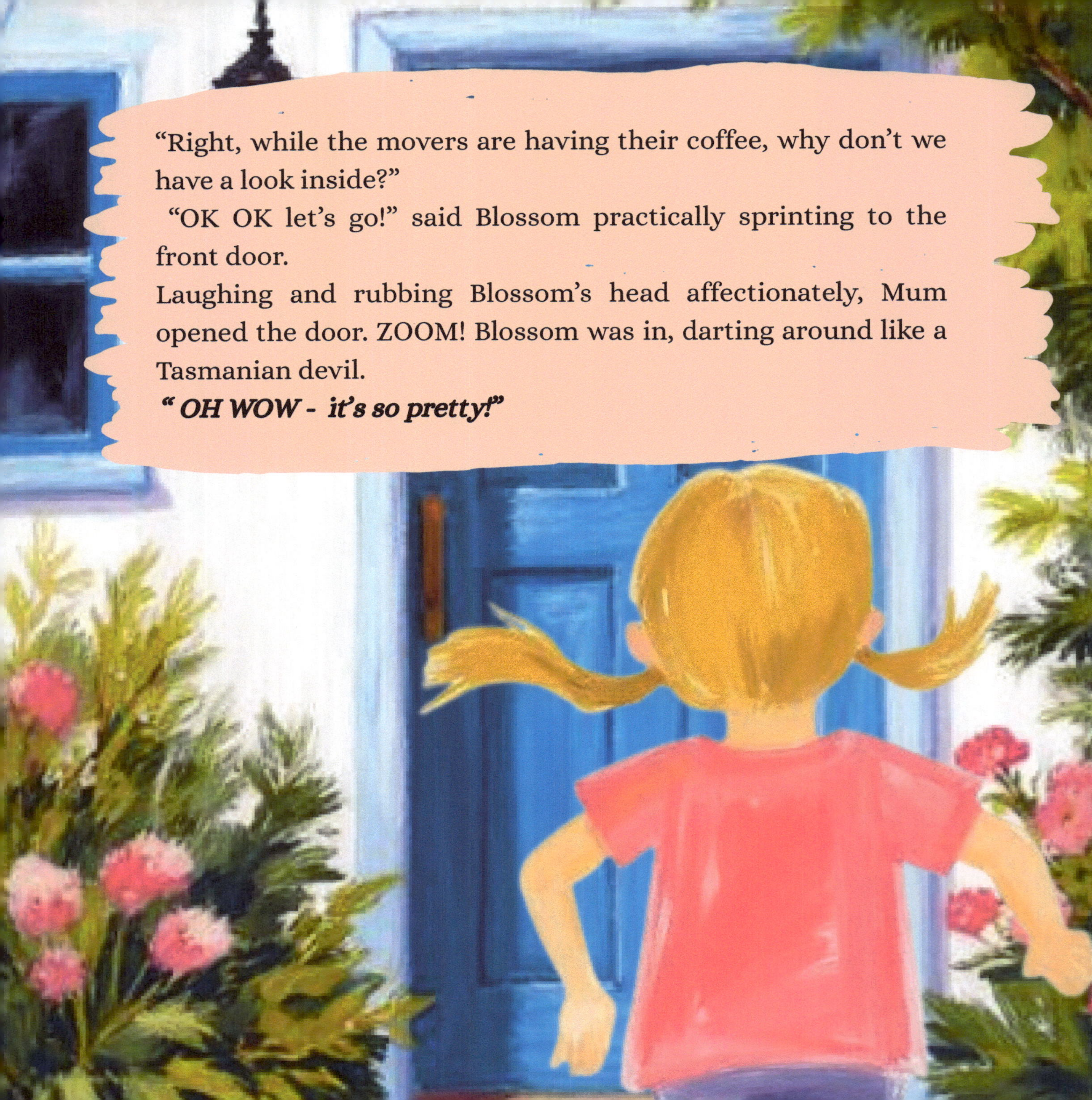

"Right, while the movers are having their coffee, why don't we have a look inside?"

"OK OK let's go!" said Blossom practically sprinting to the front door.

Laughing and rubbing Blossom's head affectionately, Mum opened the door. ZOOM! Blossom was in, darting around like a Tasmanian devil.

"OH WOW - it's so pretty!"

It was.

Very pretty.

With all the charm of the town outside. The living room had a stone fireplace perfect for roasting marshmallows and beams on the ceilings that made it feel like a fairytale house. The stairs *weren't* open but that was okay, the kitchen had an island in it (perfect for hiding behind and scaring Mum) – not a bad trade off at all!

Skipping upstairs two at a time Blossom went to the bathroom first. The bath had feet. *IT HAD FEET,* the bathroom was very small, but the bath had feet!

"Sweetheart, don't you want to see your room?" Mum called to her. "COMING!" she yelled. Standing outside the door, she took a deep breath and pushed it open.

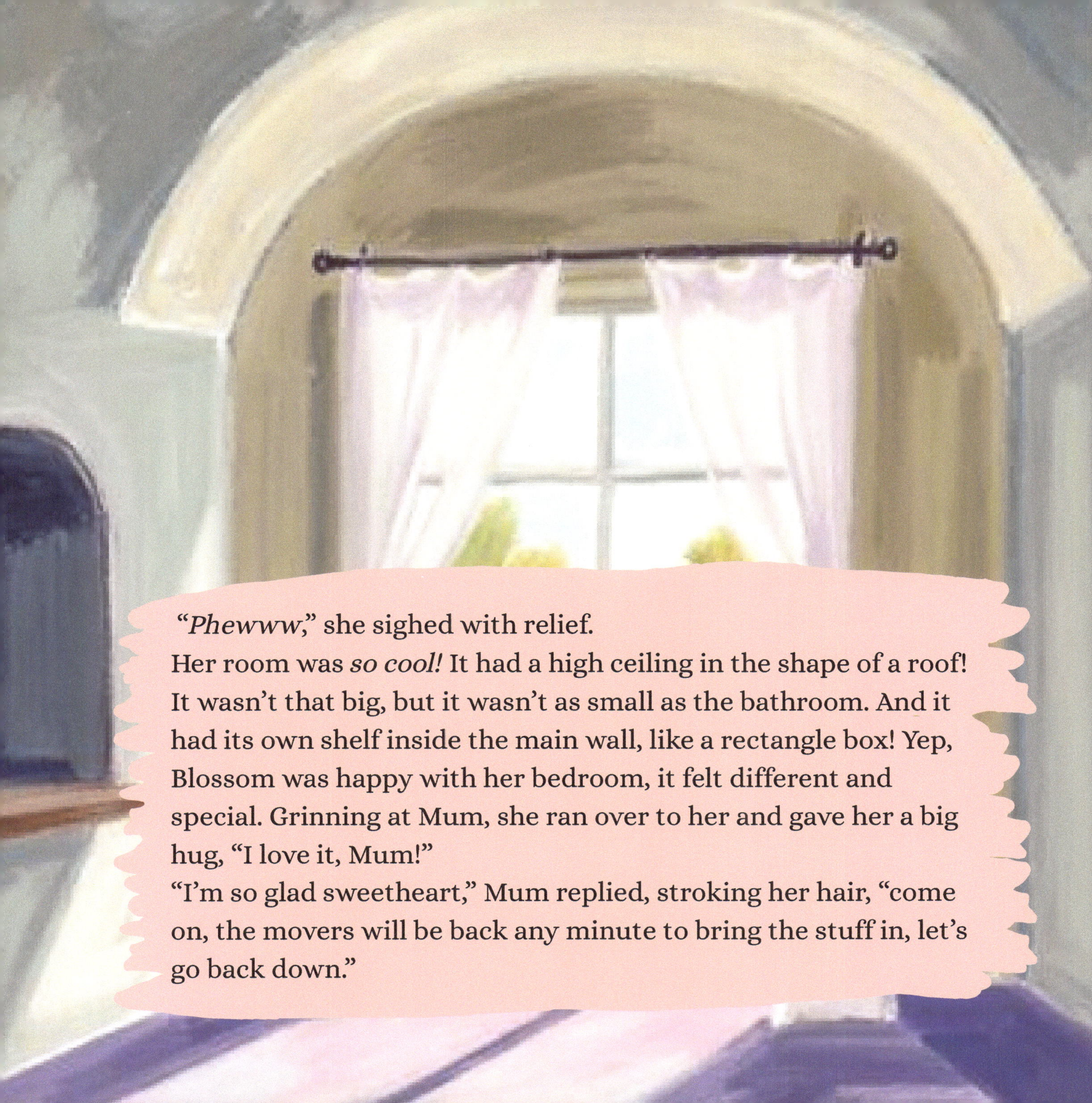

"*Phewww*," she sighed with relief.
Her room was *so cool!* It had a high ceiling in the shape of a roof! It wasn't that big, but it wasn't as small as the bathroom. And it had its own shelf inside the main wall, like a rectangle box! Yep, Blossom was happy with her bedroom, it felt different and special. Grinning at Mum, she ran over to her and gave her a big hug, "I love it, Mum!"
"I'm so glad sweetheart," Mum replied, stroking her hair, "come on, the movers will be back any minute to bring the stuff in, let's go back down."

Over the next few days, Blossom and Mum were kept very busy settling in and finding the right place for everything. It had been lots of fun, dancing around with the music blaring, rummaging through boxes for this and that, laughing at Mum dragging furniture from one place to another just to put it back where she started. Fun, but very tiring!

Finally on the fourth day everything had found it's place.

"We did it, whew!" said Blossom flopping onto the sofa in her favourite pink pyjamas.

"We did," Mum laughed, "but I do seem to recall someone being on video call to her cousins most of the time!"

"I had to Mum - first they needed to see the house. *Then* I had to tell them about the school visit. *And* they made new characters for their videos I had to see!"

"I know, I know, I was just teasing sweetheart. Come on, time for bed."

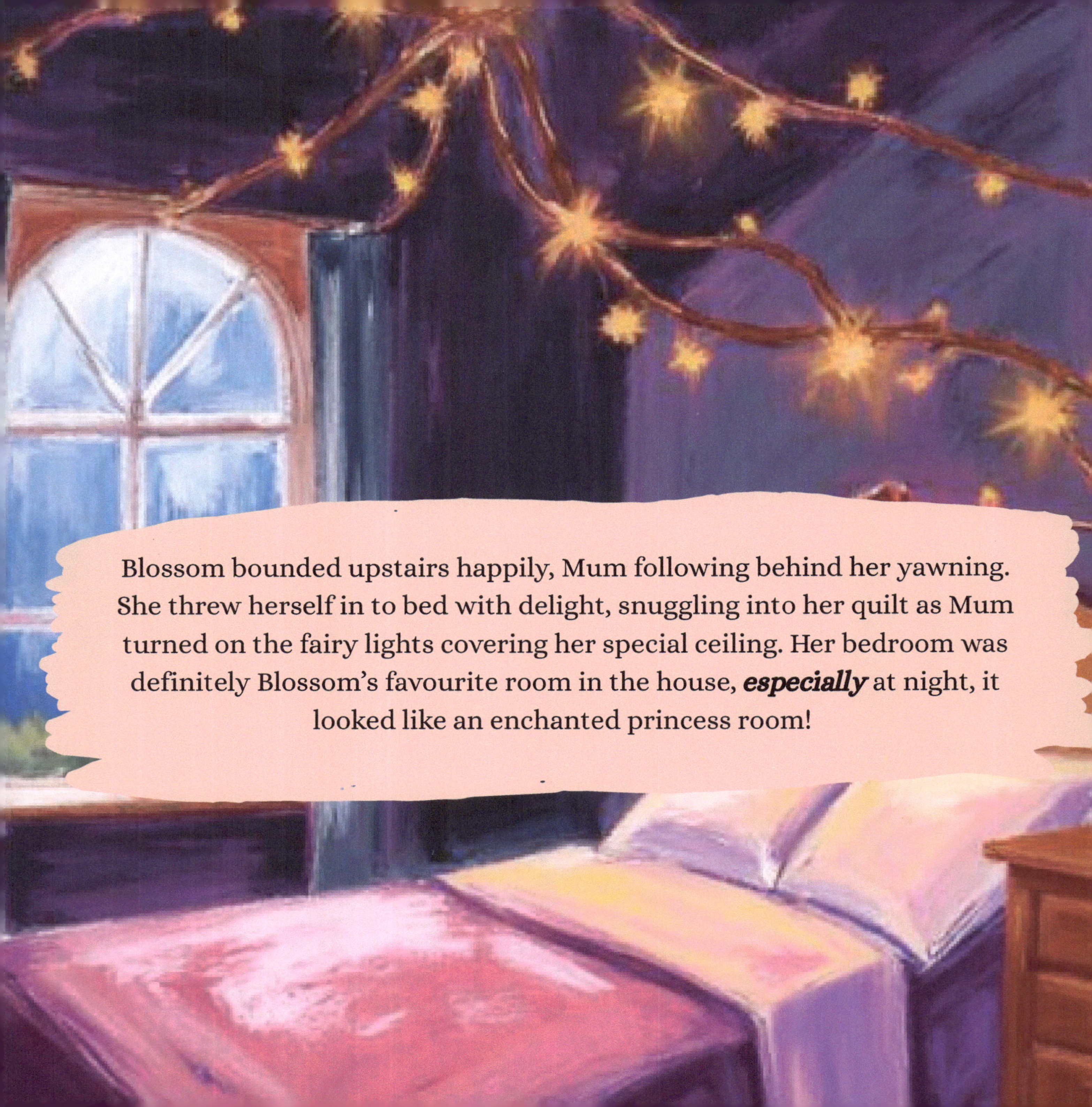

Blossom bounded upstairs happily, Mum following behind her yawning. She threw herself in to bed with delight, snuggling into her quilt as Mum turned on the fairy lights covering her special ceiling. Her bedroom was definitely Blossom's favourite room in the house, ***especially*** at night, it looked like an enchanted princess room!

As Mum settled in beside her and began reading, Blossom thought to herself that even though she DID miss the old house, this one was just as special. It had its own magic, and she couldn't wait to explore it all and make new favourite memories.

Her school visit had been *so* exciting, and she wasn't nervous *at all* about starting. Everyone they had met so far had been so friendly, she was really looking forward to making friends. Laying there cuddled into Mum, Blossom felt completely relaxed, she was asleep before Mum was halfway through the story.

The next afternoon, after a well-earned slow morning and tasty lunch, there was a knock at the door. Blossom and Mum walked over together and opened it curiously.

"HI!" said a very excited girl about the same age as Blossom. "We're your neighbours, I'm Zara! This is my mum! We're going to the park do you want to come?!?!"
"HI!!!!! I'm Blossom, you can call me LB! Can we mum? CAN WE?!" Blossom half shouted, already spinning around to grab her shoes.
"Of course we can," chuckled Mum, slipping her coat and shoes on.
"YEAH!" both girls yelled happily.

The mums smiled at each other and laughed; Mum grabbed
Blossom's jacket and locked the door.
Blossom and Zara were off, Zara leading the way and Blossom
following happily.

Smiling from ear-to-ear, filled with excitement, Blossom skipped off to the park, with her new friend, the mums nattering away behind them, *so glad* that they came on this new adventure.

LITTLE BLOSSOM'S BOOKS SERIES

BOOK 1   LITTLE BLOSSOM'S BIG DREAMS

BOOK 2   LITTLE BLOSSOM'S BIG MOVE

BOOK 3 COMING SOON!!

ISBN 978-1-9192887-2-7